M000306764

Mother, Where Are Your Teeth?

Mother, Where Are Your Teeth?

Parenting a Parent with Dementia

Trudy Way

RESOURCE *Publications* · Eugene, Oregon

MOTHER, WHERE ARE YOUR TEETH?
Parenting a Parent with Dementia

Copyright © 2016 Trudy Way. All rights reserved. Except for brief
quotations in critical publications or reviews, no part of this book
may be reproduced in any manner without prior written per-
mission from the publisher. Write: Permissions, Wipf and Stock
Publishers, 199 W. 8th Ave., Suite 3, Eugene, OR 97401.

Resource Publications
An Imprint of Wipf and Stock Publishers
199 W. 8th Ave., Suite 3
Eugene, OR 97401

www.wipfandstock.com

PAPERBACK ISBN: 978-1-4982-9853-7
HARDCOVER ISBN: 978-1-4982-5138-9
EBOOK ISBN: 978-1-4982-9854-4

Manufactured in the U.S.A.

In memory of my mother

Helen O'Meara

Epigraph

I LOVE WRITING. IN fiction I love the way characters tell you what they want to say and do. In writing memoir, you write what happened to you. You relive the scenes vividly, harshly, sadly, or lovingly, as they were. In the writing and reliving of this story, there was a perspective that made me wish I could have been kinder, more understanding, and more loving. Writing it was a painful process. I did it to offer my experience to you, in hopes that on your journey you'll know that you are doing the best that you can, just as I did.

Blessings, Trudy Way

Contents

Introduction

If you've picked up this book then you are probably entering a new phase of your life—parenting your parent—though this book can be helpful for any loved one with dementia. If you don't understand why an elderly parent has become difficult, or is doing odd things, they may be showing signs of dementia. However, other things like dehydration or drugs can cause strange behaviors too, so rule out those possibilities first with a check-up from your doctor.

I am not a physician and I don't claim to be an authority on dementia, but I took care of both of my parents who suffered with dementia. Sharing experiences can help in ways that statistics and studies can't. Sometimes you just need someone who understands what you are going through. If that's what you are looking for, then this book may be helpful, because caring for a loved one is stressful and all-consuming.

My father developed dementia first. I didn't recognize it then, and I didn't recognize it years later, when my mother showed signs of it. Not everyone who has dementia is difficult. Unfortunately, my parents were.

When elder parents pass away it is sad, but it is tragic when they morph into someone unrecognizable. It helps if we don't take it personally, and that is a challenge. It can also be a great learning experience.

This is the story of my mother and me as we plummeted into the world of dementia.

Chapter 1

An Unexpected Shock

My step-father, Tom was in the hospital. He had heart problems. He was doing better and was scheduled to go home the following day. Instead, he died.

His family came as soon as they heard. Mother didn't want them to go the mortuary to see his body before he was cremated. I didn't understand why, and when I tried to reason with her, she flew into a rage. His son and daughter wanted to honor my mother's wishes but they also wanted to pay their last respects to their father. I told them that they should do what they wanted to do. After all, he was their father. I attributed her unreasonableness to the shock of her husband's unexpected death.

Mother hired a large boat to scatter Tom's ashes in the Pacific Ocean. It was a good farewell with his buddies toasting him with a shot of whiskey as the cloud of ashes settled on the water. Mother surprised me with her good spirits that day.

A couple of days later, after everyone had gone home, mother asked me to come over. My mother had a strong personality, but now she seemed vulnerable, something that I'd never seen in her before. She wanted me to be a co-signer on her bank accounts and her safe deposit box. We went to two banks, one where she had certificates of deposit, and the other, where her checking, savings, and safe deposit box were. She didn't want me to know any of her financial affairs beyond that. I understood and honored her wishes. She had always been perfectly capable of managing her own money. Looking back, I'm grateful for that window of vulnerability, otherwise what was to come would have been even more difficult.

Chapter 2

Pearls

AS MOTHER SETTLED INTO her new life without her husband, our visits became more relaxed. We had about six good years before I noticed any odd behavior. Even then, when she'd do or say something strange, I'd brush it off thinking it was just a bad day, or she was getting old and forgetful. But one incident, between my mother and my cousin Diane, really confused me. It involved a strand of pearls.

"Aunt Helen is upset with me" my cousin told me, "I don't know what I did. When I call her, she picks up the phone and as soon as she hears my voice, she hangs up."

My mother loved Diane, they had always gotten along great. I thought mother might be confused, thinking it was a telemarketer. I called her and repeated the story Diane had told me.

"That's right," mother said.

"But why?"

"She stole my pearls. I called the police and they agreed with me."

"Oh, Mother, Diane would never steal anything from you. She loves you."

"Sure, Trudy, take her side." The phone went dead. I called her back three times. She wouldn't answer. I brought it up again when I saw her, but I was never able to convince her about the pearls. I couldn't understand it, and my cousin was hurt.

Chapter 3

Dog Washing

A YEAR AFTER MY mother's husband died, I surprised her with a cocker spaniel puppy. It was the first gift from me that she was really thrilled with. It made me happy. She named the dog Katie, and they quickly settled in together. My mother showered her with love. It was a side of my mother I was unfamiliar with.

Katie grew to be a beautiful dog with a silky coat the color of honey. Her large brown eyes were fringed in wispy lashes. Mother was proud of her. For years she never missed Katie's monthly trip to the groomers, so I was surprised one day when I noticed Katie looking shaggy. When I asked mother about it she said she'd been meaning to make an appointment for her but she'd been busy. She'd call next week. The following week she said the same thing. I wondered if it was becoming difficult for her. I suggested that she and I take Katie to the groomer together.

"Forget it Trudy. I'll take care of it."

"I didn't mean to interfere Mother, I just thought I could help."

"Nip it," she said, taking a long drag on her cigarette.

I couldn't understand why she was procrastinating. Katie's fur was matting and if I tried to pet her she'd yelp. I knew it was painful.

When I arrived the following week, Katie was worse. I gave my mother an ultimatum, "Call for an appointment or I will take her myself."

"Stop runnin' on me," she yelled.

It was late morning and already hot when I reached mother's house the following week, so we decided on an early lunch at one of our favorite restaurants.

When we returned, I waited until mother had settled into her chair. We were both complaining about the heat so I felt it was a perfect segue into my agenda.

"I think I'll give Katie a bath today," I said, "it will cool her down."

"Oh no, you're not. I'm taking her to the groomers myself."

"You've promised that for weeks Mother, but you never do it."

"Oh Trudy leave me alone, you're always runnin' on me."

"Mother, I . . . "

"Come here, Katie," she said. Katie jumped into her lap. "You're my good girl," she cooed. Then she picked up the newspaper and shut me out.

I couldn't understand why she was acting so unpleasant when I was only trying to help.

I went into the garage where she kept the dog supplies. I found a bottle of shampoo covered in dust in a bucket, and a dog brush on a shelf. I was looking for a towel when I heard the deadbolt click. I tried the door. It was locked. "Mother?"

She didn't answer.

I waited a minute, then knocked on the door.

"Mother, please open the door." I stood in disbelief. I knew I could get out of the big garage door if I had to. But I was afraid that once I got out she'd close it and I'd be stuck outside without my purse and keys to my car.

I pounded on the door. "Mother!"

Finally, I heard the lock click. I turned the door knob. mother was standing there, blocking my way.

"You're not going to shampoo Katie. I'll do it myself," she said.

"Too late. I'm doing it now."

When I tried to pick Katie up, mother hit me with the leash.

"Stop it! What's wrong with you? I'm just giving her a bath. Her fur is matted. It hurts her."

Katie didn't know what to do. She looked back and forth between us. I picked her up. Mother tried to pull her out of my arms. She finally gave up and stormed down the hall to her bedroom. I took Katie outside. I wasn't sure if she'd let me wash her; she could be snappy and she was upset. But she didn't struggle or try to leave. She stood with her head low. The day was hot. The sun bore down on us.

I tried to comb the mats out of Katie's fur, but they were beyond that. I had to cut them out, which was difficult because they were close to her skin, and my hands were shaking. Tears blurred my vision. I didn't know if they were because Katie was being so good, or because my mother had been so mean.

It took me over an hour, and when I finished, Katie was happy. She ran around and around in the yard and then up to the sliding glass door, her whole body wiggling. Mother was sitting in her chair smoking. I tried to open the door, but now it was locked.

"Mother," I said forcing myself to sound cheerful, "Katie wants to see you. Please open the door."

She glared at me.

"Please," I begged, "unlock the door."

Katie and I stood side by side, both of us pressed against the glass. My mother lounged in her chair, her legs crossed on the footstool. She looked at us as she blew long shafts of cigarette smoke in the air. Perspiration soaked my clothes. My hair stuck to my face. When she finished her cigarette she slowly snubbed it out in the ashtray. She got out of her chair and opened the door. She took Katie in her arms and with the air of a victor, marched down the hall to her bedroom and slammed the door shut.

I couldn't move; I felt like a cement block. I forced myself to breathe. Deep breaths, in and out. Finally, my shoulders let down and my body softened. Tears swelled in my eyes. It was time to go home.

On the freeway I leaned my head out the car window; my hair whipped in every direction. I stayed there until the wind beat the smell of mother's cigarette smoke off of me and my tears dried up.

Chapter 4

Bills

MONTHS PASSED BEFORE ANOTHER episode. Then one day, I saw that Mother's bills were lying on the table in the same place I'd seen them on my last visit.

"Wow, Mom, you've got a serious pile of mail there. Do you want me to sort through it for you?"

"I don't need your help, Trudy." She flicked her cigarette in the ashtray. "Just leave things alone."

"I'm not trying to interfere, Mother, I just thought I might help."

"Right," she said.

Was she being sarcastic?

A few weeks later, I mentioned that the table was practically invisible with all the mail stacked on top of it.

"Stay out of my business," she snapped.

When she left the room, I grabbed a pile of mail and stuffed it into my purse. I felt guilty doing it, but I was worried that bills like her car insurance, homeowner's insurance, or property taxes wouldn't get paid. When I got home, I separated the bills from the junk mail and made files. A few of her bills were overdue, so I paid them.

When mother's bank statement came, I pounced on it. After her husband died, she'd bought new living room and bedroom furniture. I was happy for her. She had everything just the way she liked it. But, I thought she had more money than I was seeing in her account. Besides that,

I saw a check for two new iron gates for her backyard. I was surprised she'd replaced the wooden ones because they provided privacy and were still in good condition. The new ones were pricey. She told me that her neighbor said iron gates were better, because the police could see into her yard when they were patrolling. Police patrolling? In her bedroom community?

I found a check for tree trimming. She had three orange trees in her backyard that hadn't been trimmed for years. When I questioned her about it, she was vague. I was concerned that someone had taken advantage of her. I called the tree trimmer and he told me that he'd trimmed several large trees. I threatened to turn him in for taking advantage of my aging mother, since she had no large trees, and the three trees she did have, had not been trimmed. Caught in a lie, he was apologetic. I told him I wanted the money returned. He came to the house. The man was nervous and I could see that he felt bad. We compromised, he would clear out the side yard, which was full of old wood and junk, and I would let it drop.

Mother was writing checks for things that she didn't need and ignoring her bills. My husband agreed to talk to her. He always seemed to calm her down, whereas anything I said ignited her. When he called, she told him she was doing fine financially. No problems. She was unconcerned. He made her promise that if she needed help in the future, she'd let him know. She still had her certificates of deposits and maybe she had other accounts that we weren't aware of.

A couple of months later, she surprised me by saying that I could take care of her bills. I couldn't believe my ears. I quickly gathered everything up before she changed her mind. At home I spread out all of the invoices on my dinning room table. Her house and car were paid off, but she still had to pay the insurance for both of them, plus property taxes, a daily newspaper, gas, food, utilities, vet and grooming bills for her dog, a gardener and occasional trips to the hair salon for perms. When I added it all up against her Social Security benefits, and her small pension, it wasn't enough. She was dipping into her savings every month just to keep up. It wouldn't be long before she had no savings left and then she'd go through her CDs. The fragility of life washed over me.

Chapter 5

Driver's License

STILL STINGING FROM THE dog washing incident, I stayed away from mother for awhile until the guilt got the best of me. When I finally saw her she was in good spirits and seemingly without any resentment. But this was her way. She would never talk about her feelings. I'd grown up that way. Why, then, was I so emotional?

Now I had to address her driving, something I dreaded. I knew she hadn't passed her eye test when she'd gone to get her license renewed months ago. She did see her eye doctor who removed a cataract. It surprised me that she'd taken care of it so quickly. It made me feel like she was on top of things. But, since the operation, she hadn't gone back to the DMV. At least I didn't think she had.

Mother was still driving, mostly to the grocery store and back, which was only a few blocks away. I wasn't comfortable with it, but I didn't say anything. I didn't want to upset her. I talked my worries over with my husband constantly, until he finally convinced me that the problem wasn't going away. I had to face it and do the right thing.

Mother and I went out for lunch. She had a hamburger with pickles, her favorite lunch. I had no appetite. I knew I had to talk to her about her car. I didn't want to be a nagging daughter, and I certainly wasn't up for another big fight. I felt sorry for her and at the same time I was terrified of what her reaction was going to be. My stomach tightened.

When we got back to her house I fixed us both a cup of coffee and sat down across from her.

"Did you ever get your driver's license renewed?" I asked casually.

She lit a cigarette and dealt herself a hand of solitaire on the small table in front of her chair.

"Mother?"

"Stop runnin' on me."

"Mother, be nice." I took a sip of coffee, but my hand was shaking and coffee slopped on my blouse. You know you can't drive with an expired license."

"I'm not."

"May I see your license?"

"No, you can't."

I waited, trying to let the tension lose some of its force before I continued. It was quiet except for the slap of her cards on the table as she played her game.

"Mother, you realize you will not be covered by insurance if your license isn't valid." I didn't know if this was true, but I said it anyway.

Slap slap went her cards.

"What if you hit someone? You could get sued and lose your house."

"Oh, Trudy, mind your own beeswax."

I went into the kitchen for a glass of water, and to pull my hair out. I needed time to regain my composure. I heard her walking down the hall. As soon as the bathroom door closed, I ran for her purse on the table. I felt like a purse snatcher but I had to find her license before she came back. I prayed for the slight possibility that her license was valid, but it had expired. Of course it had. Deep down I'd known that. Not really even that deep down. I just didn't want to face it or face her. I didn't want to be the one to take away my mother's freedom.

When I heard her coming back. My mouth went dry. I fumbled to get her license back in her wallet and her wallet back in her purse and her purse back on the table before she caught me.

When she had settled in her chair, I asked to see her license. I felt like a snake.

"Nip it," she said.

I handed her her purse. Her jaw clenched. Her eyes narrowed. She didn't move. Neither did I. Finally, she opened her purse, fumbled her license out of her wallet and threw it at me.

"There," she yelled, "you don't believe me? Look for yourself."

I knew what I was going to find. Didn't she know it too?

"Mother, I . . . I'm sorry," I stammered, "this has expired."

She pulled herself off the chair and grabbed her driver's license out of my hand. She tried to stuff it back into her wallet, but she was so furious that she threw her wallet at me instead.

I tried to keep my voice calm. "Let's go to the DMV right now and you can get a booklet to study for your test."

"Forget it Trudy. You always want to run my life. You think you're so perfect. You know everything."

This wasn't fun for either of us. I felt awful, but I'd ignored it for as long as I could. I didn't understand why she wouldn't let me take her to the DMV to get the booklet. For now, I decided I had no choice. I took her car keys. When she saw what I was doing she lunged at me grabbing for the keys. When she couldn't get them, she marched down the hall to her bedroom, and slammed the door behind her. I left for home in tears.

My husband Ron and I visited her a few days later to disable her car. Mother was cool to me, but I had to keep the conversation going to give Ron time to remove the battery cables. I felt like I was dismantling my mother's life, inch by inch. I was miserable.

After that, whenever I offered to take her to get her license renewed she'd decline, which made me wonder if she was a little unsure of herself too. Her four-door, white Taurus, was retired to the garage. The air in the tires slowly seeped out. She never mentioned her car again.

Chapter 6

Groceries and Cleaning Lady

Since mother couldn't drive anymore, I told her to plan on me coming every Thursday. I lived a little over an hour away, so I would get there before noon, and we'd go out to lunch and then take care of whatever chores she needed help with. Having lunch out with mother was nice for both of us, plus I could get away from the smell of cigarette smoke that permeated her house.

About six months later I noticed more changes in her. At lunch she wasn't interested in talking, instead she'd stare off at the people around us. I tried asking her questions about her childhood, but she'd always say she didn't remember or give me a one-word answer. I racked my brain to find things she might find interesting to talk about. Nothing helped. When lunch was over I was exhausted.

Afterward, I took her shopping for groceries. The two essential purchases for her were cigarettes and wine. At first I bought just a few bottles, but her neighbor told me that she was borrowing wine from her every week. She was concerned that mother would fall because she was unsteady, shuffling and teetering her way across the street. I was concerned too, and I didn't want her mooching off her neighbors. After that, I bought seven bottles of wine, thinking it would be more than enough. The following week I found seven empty bottles in the trash. One bottle of wine, every evening, for a ninety-eight-pound octogenarian was excessive. What was I to do?

Mother had smoked all my life. She had a cigarette in her hand, her mouth, or an ashtray at all times. She and her house reeked of cigarette smoke. I hated cigarettes but if I didn't get her enough to last the week, then she'd stumble her way to the grocery store. It was an arduous trek for her. So I bought several cartons of cigarettes at a time. I wanted to tell the grocer that the cigarettes weren't for me. I didn't want to buy them. I thought they were disgusting, but I had to for my mother. Instead, I kept my mouth shut and paid the bill.

I stocked mother's refrigerator with juices, lunch meats, cheese, bread, bacon, eggs, peanut butter, blueberry preserves, baked potatoes, wrapped and ready to cook in the microwave, frozen snacks, and TV dinners. Easy things I thought she'd like. I knew she liked cereal so I got an assortment pack, and of course coffee.

The following week almost none of the food had been touched. After a few weeks it was easy to see her favorites. Chicken and noodle TV dinners, peanut butter and jelly sandwiches, Wheaties, Breakfast of Champs (she always said it that way), and coffee.

Mother cooked her TV dinners in the oven. I told her it would be faster in the microwave, but she didn't seem to understand how the microwave worked anymore. I went over it with her several times, but she never used it.

I tried to introduce new things that were easy to make, but she wouldn't touch them. She had her favorites and never seemed to tire of them.

Mother had always kept a clean house, but lately her furniture nearly groaned under the weight of dust layering it day after day. Not only that, but dust bunnies the size of mice rolled back and forth across the floor until they caught on the legs of furniture or the dog's paws. I started coming earlier every week so that I could clean. But, between the cleaning, lunch, grocery shopping, chores, and driving an hour each way, I was worn out.

"I can do it myself," mother said, when I suggested a cleaning lady. Hadn't she noticed that I'd been doing it?

There was a limit to how dirty I was going to let her house get before I put my foot down. When I told her the housekeeper would be my treat, she finally agreed. Then she began to worry that the woman would steal from her while we were at lunch.

I was anxious waiting for the cleaning lady to show up for the first time. Mother was hiding her jewelry. I was worried she'd change her mind at the last minute. When the woman arrived, her husband was with her. She explained that they worked together. I held my breath, but mother took this new information easily, and though she still had an eagle-eye on the woman, she had nothing but smiles for the husband, engaging him in conversation and making little jokes.

When we returned the house looked spotless. I was grateful that this chore was off my list. But after a few weeks the cleaning lady took me aside and pointed out cigarette burns on the sheets and on mother's chair in the living room.

This was unsettling but I knew she'd never stop smoking. I needed help. I began seeing a therapist. He was a small man, a former Franciscan Monk, near my mother's age. He had on black slacks and a dark blue sweater over a white button-down shirt.

"I don't think she's safe living alone anymore," I lamented, "but I can't just drag her out of her house. What can I do?"

"I can see how worried you are about your mother," he said softly. "This isn't an easy time, but you're stronger than you think. Trust your instincts," he said. "You'll know when a change has to be made and then you'll be clear about the next step. If you're not clear about what to do now, then you have to be patient until you are. Everything has its time."

He was quiet then. His hands were folded in his lap as if waiting for the words he'd just spoken to find their way to me.

Chapter 7

Bank Incident

MOTHER'S ONLY INCOME WAS Social Security and a very small pension. Her Social Security checks began to pile up on the shelf in the kitchen. I offered to take her to the bank to deposit them after lunch.

"I can do it myself," she flared.

"You can't drive. How will you get there?"

"My neighbor Don will take me."

"Mother, why bother a neighbor when I can take you?"

She took a drag on her cigarette and glared at me. "You're always runnin' on me."

On my visit the following week, I slipped mother's Social Security checks into my purse when she wasn't looking. After lunch I swung by her bank and pulled into a parking place. Before she could say anything, I pulled the checks out and told her that I'd brought them along because I thought she'd want to deposit them into her account. She grabbed the checks out of my hand. Her eyebrows pinched together as she glared at me. I held my breath. When sufficient anger had been dealt to me through her squinty eyes, she opened the car door and made her way into the bank.

The following month she said, "Can we drop by the bank after lunch? I have a deposit I'd like to make."

"Sure," I said, suppressing a smile.

The bank was chock-full of people and my mother commented that it must be payday. We got in the long line, waiting our turn and that's when I saw that she didn't have her check, she had the stub.

"Where is your check?" She held up the stub.

"That isn't a check, Mother."

"Leave me alone," she shrieked, "and mind your own business." Everyone in the bank turned to look at us. My face shot hot.

"Mother, you don't have to yell at me," I whispered.

"Well, you just keep runnin' on me," she said, still loud enough to be heard by the people around us.

Perspiration ran down my sides.

When it was her turn, mother marched up to the teller with the stub in her hand. I walked up with her. She elbowed me to the side, then hunched her shoulder up to guard me from seeing anything.

A woman slipped up next to me and whispered that she was sorry, and that her mother was the same way too. "Hang in there," she said. My chin quivered. I was grateful for her kindness. I needed it right then.

"I'm sorry madam, this is the stub, do you have the check?" the teller asked, pushing the stub towards mother.

Mother pulled herself up as close as she could to the teller's face.

"I'll have you know," she said, her voice echoing throughout the lobby, "that I worked for the Bank of America for 30 years and I certainly know a check when I see one."

She shoved the stub back to the teller. Mother's face was fierce. The teller's expression didn't change. She said she was sorry, but she couldn't help. Mother grabbed the stub. Her eyes narrowed, she pinched her lips, and for a moment I thought she might take a swing at the teller. Thankfully, she turned and marched out of the bank, puffed up, full of indignation. I trailed behind.

From then on, when I knew her Social Security check would be arriving, I tried to get to the mailbox before she did. I was afraid she would throw the check away and keep the stub, which she must have done with this check. I wanted her to call the Social Security office about the lost check, but she refused.

"Oh, Trudy, it isn't lost." Then she'd shake her head at me like I'd lost my mind.

Chapter 8

Cherry Tree

I NOTICED MOTHER HAD something odd on her arm. On closer inspection I saw that she had cut the foot off of a white sock and pulled the top up her forearm.

"Why are you wearing that, Mother?"

"It's a bandage."

I could see a little blood stain on it and pulled it away to have a look. She had a big gash on her arm.

"Mother, what happened?" My voice was shrill.

"Nothing," she said.

"Nothing? Look. You've hurt yourself."

"Oh, this," she said, "I fell out of a cherry tree." She yanked the sock back up.

She didn't have a cherry tree. I looked at her, not knowing what to say. But she didn't expect a response, she was uninterested.

I went to get a Band-Aid and that's when I saw water in the hall. I followed it into the bathroom.

"Mother." I yelled, running into the living room. "Did you know there is water all over your bathroom floor and out into the hall?

"Don't worry," she said, taking a drag on her cigarette, "someone turned the faucet on in the middle of the night. It overflowed."

I looked back at the water in the hall and then at her and her sock-wrapped arm. I decided to keep my mouth shut and clean it up. When I was done I brought a Band-Aid and a tube of antiseptic out to clean and wrap her gash. She jerked away.

"It's fine, Trudy. Leave me alone." She hoisted the sock back into place. She seemed pleased with it.

Mother had always been fastidious about herself. But lately stains dotted the front of her blouses and pants. Her closets were packed with clothes so that wasn't the problem.

"Why don't you put on another blouse Mother, that one is stained."

"Forget it," she said.

"Are you sure? I know you have that pretty . . . "

"Forget it Trudy," she said with a cigarette clenched between her teeth. She squinted her eyes against the smoke. I could see the steely resolve in her face, and I knew our conversation was done. She snapped her newspaper up in front of her face.

I was straightening things up when I noticed the lid on her clothes hamper wide open and clothes piled high. I couldn't stuff them down enough to close the lid. I sorted the darks from the lights and bundled an armload of laundry to throw into the washing machine. When she saw me, she flew out of her chair.

"Stop it," she yelled, grabbing at the clothes.

"Mother, why are you upset, I'm going to put them into the washing machine."

"Put them back. I'll take care of them." She pulled at the clothes.

"I have them all ready to go; can't I just do one load?"

"Oh, Trudy, why are you're runnin' on me again? Can't you just leave my things alone?"

She was so upset that I put everything back. It was hard to know what she needed help with and what she could do on her own. I didn't want to make her feel incompetent. And I didn't want to take over her life, I only wanted to help.

But in a few weeks she didn't have any clean clothes left. Even her canvas shoes had stains on them.

So when she picked up the newspaper, I snuck down the hall with an armload of clothes hugged to my chest on my way to the washing machine. I held my breath as I peeked around each corner.

When the clothes were dry, I folded them as fast as I could and hurried them back to her room. I knew my fear of being detected was out of proportion, but I never knew what would set her off. I didn't want another run-in with her.

She never asked how the clean clothes reappeared in her closet and drawers, nor did she notice the hamper at the end of the hall with the lid closed.

Chapter 9

The Fire

I WAS GOING ON a trip for a couple of days and I stopped by to see mother on the way to the airport. When I walked in the front door I noticed black cobwebs in the entry way. It was just after Halloween and my mother loved Halloween so I thought maybe they were decorations. But as I got farther into the house I saw black cobwebs and soot everywhere. Hadn't the cleaning lady noticed this? When I walked into the kitchen I stopped in my tracks. The wall by the stove was burned black and parts of the stove had melted. I flew into the living room where Mother was watching TV.

"Mother, did you have a fire?"

"Yes," she said, "a picture blew up, but I put it out."

"A picture? What picture?"

"Oh Trudy, don't start runnin' on me."

"Mother, you had a fire. The house could have burned down." My voice was shrill, but I couldn't help it.

"Well, it didn't, did it." she said. She turned back to her TV and patted her dog.

There was a TV dinner burned to a crisp in her oven and an uncooked one beside it. What now? I couldn't just leave. She had averted disaster this time, but she was lucky.

I called her neighbor who came over and turned off the gas to the stove. Then I called Jean, mother's step-daughter, to see if she would come and stay with mother while I was gone. She agreed. We thought everything was covered, but when I got home Jean told me she hadn't stayed at the house even one night. She said when she arrived mother was very nice and they had a good visit. But when she went into the bedroom to go to bed, mother threw the door opened and told her to get the hell out of her house or she was going to call the cops. Jean had never seen this side of my mother. It scared her. She tried to calm her down, but nothing worked. Mother was in a rage. Finally, Jean left.

She came back the next day, for a couple of hours in the morning, and then again in the evening, to bring her dinner. It was a hardship for her, but she didn't know what else to do.

Later, when I questioned my mother about Jean, she wouldn't talk about it.

Then I knew, mother had crossed a line. It was time to make some changes for her. It had been almost seven years since her husband had died.

Chapter 10

Moving

Moving mother out of her house wasn't going to be easy. I had no Power of Attorney. No rights. I had to prove mother was unsafe living by herself. I made an appointment with a doctor who would do tests for dementia. How I got her to go still amazes me.

I had written a letter beforehand, outlining Mother's fire and other troubling incidents, which I handed to the nurse surreptitiously. Mother seemed completely normal. Now, I was worried that they would think I was the one who was nuts.

They asked my mother questions: What is the date today? Who is the president of the United States? What month is it? Simple daily things. I wasn't sure of the date and mother didn't know it either. She did know the president. When they asked her to subtract 3 numbers from 100 backward, going as far as she could, I went into panic because I'm lousy at math. Mother got a few right and I was impressed. Now I was beginning to worry about myself.

Next, the nurse named three things and told her to remember them. I was mentally repeating them over in my mind. She said she'd come back to those three things later to see if mother remembered them. I was unnerved, I couldn't remember the last one already. I tend to panic in situations where something is required of me, whereas, my mother is usually unruffled. But, she couldn't remember any of the words.

She was asked to draw a clock and place the numbers in their correct positions. She couldn't do it. The next test was to replicate a simple drawing. It was just a few lines. She started and then stopped. She couldn't do that either. I felt awful for her, worried that she was embarrassed not being able to do these simple things, but she didn't seem concerned.

Mother still read the newspaper so she knew what was going on locally, if not in the world, and she could carry on a conversation, even making little jokes, but the tests that she failed were significant. The doctor said that Mother was showing signs of dementia. I was mortified when he said this in front of her, but again, she didn't seem to be bothered by it.

An appointment with a social worker was set up to visit mother in her home. When the woman arrived, mother was cool to her. The woman was pleasant and tried to engage her in a conversation, but mother lit a cigarette and puffed leisurely, as if neither of us were there. Then, without warning, she turned to the woman and shouted: "Listen bitch, you better get the hell out of my house before I call the police."

I nearly jumped out of my chair. The woman's eyes popped wide, but she kept her cool. She tried a few more questions, but mother was enraged. She got out of her chair and looked like she was going to hit the woman. I grabbed her arm and she jerked free, then stormed off to her bedroom.

Very soon I got the papers that I could move her out of her home. But, how would I do it?

Thanksgiving was in a few days, and we planned to have a family dinner at our house. I thought it would be a good time to transition her into our guest house.

My husband and I had talked about having her live in our house with us, but mother was unpredictable. I was afraid she'd turn on stove and start a fire in the middle of the night or turn the water on and forget it. I was even worried about her getting into the knives or scissors. That may sound paranoid, and maybe I was, but I'd seen such strange behavior in her that I wasn't comfortable sleeping when she was in the house.

On Thanksgiving my son, daughter-in-law, and grand children picked mother up, as they usually did, for holidays with us. I had driven to her house and parked out of sight, waiting until she left with our kids, so that I could pack some of her belongings that she'd need right away. We'd get the bulk of her things later.

We had a beautiful two-bedroom guest house on our property that we'd repainted and readied for mother. I dreaded taking her away from her home, but just like the driver's license, it had to be done. One thing I knew for sure, she wouldn't be able to smoke anymore. At her house there were cigarette burns everywhere. The most concerning was in her bed and I knew that would never change. From my earliest memories, mother had smoked in bed and she'd been smoking for over sixty years. I was sick with worry about the reaction she might have by taking her cigarettes away at this critical time in her life. The week before she arrived, I bought boxes of nicotine patches and called the company hot line for advice with hypothetical questions that hounded me constantly.

Thanksgiving dinner was a blur. I barely ate anything. I avoided any conversation with mother because I knew what was ahead. I felt like a traitor.

After dinner I asked mother if she'd like to see the guest house that we'd spruced up. She was in a happy mood after having a couple of glasses of wine and was eager to see it. My son Nick, joined me and together we helped mother along the driveway.

I said something about her staying overnight.

"No, I want to go home."

I took a deep breath. "Mother we thought it would be nice to have you live in our guest house now, so that I can help you." She stopped dead in her tracks.

"I'm going to jump off the Brooklyn Bridge," she cried. I could see the panic in her eyes. A feeling of nausea washed over me.

"Why are you taking me away from my home? Why are you doing this to me? I can take care of myself," she said. It was a plea, not a rant.

I was voiceless looking into her frightened face.

My son said, "It's a change Grammie, but it can be a good change."

She looked at me and held her chest, "I know my house isn't as grand as yours, but it's my house. My Tom is there. I love it. Can't you understand that Trudy?"

My heart splintered. Of course I understood. I hated what I was doing to my mother, but what else could I do? The truth was, she was not able to live alone any longer and she wouldn't let anyone live with her. It was one of the lowest days of my life.

Somehow my son and I got her to the guesthouse. She sat on the sofa holding her dog. We tried to talk to her but she stared ahead. Her eyes looked vacant. Suddenly she jumped up and rummaged through all of the cupboards. My son thought she was looking for cigarettes, so he put a nicotine patch on her back. It was sundown, a time of day when older people can experience behavioral problems.

For people with dementia or Alzheimer's it's called Sun-downing. Mother was clearly confused, and why wouldn't she be? I had jerked her life out from under her.

I used the patches religiously, reducing them as time went on, until she didn't need them anymore. After that, as unbelievable as it seems, she never once asked me for a cigarette. Mother had a big shock to her system. Sometimes there are no good choices. It was a heart-rending day.

Chapter 11

Mother Runs Away

THE NEXT DAY I saw mother heading out the door: hat snug on her head, purse over her arm, Katie on a leash. She walked through our backyard as I ran from window to window wondering what to do. I didn't think she'd last very long because she tired easily. I watched and waited. She got onto our long driveway, maneuvering a curb. I was amazed at what she was doing. When I couldn't see her from the house I ran outside and dodged behind trees, keeping her in my sight. I was sure she couldn't last much longer, but she seemed energized. She was on a mission.

Our house was on five acres enclosed by a split rail fence and a gate at the end of our driveway. The gate was closed. Mother marched with her nose in the air, jerking Katie whenever she tried to stop for a smell. When she reached the gate she pushed on it. When it didn't open I thought she'd turn around and come back. She didn't. Instead she disappeared behind the bushes that lined the fence. My breath caught. I ran as fast as I could down the driveway. The ground was uneven behind the bushes. I was sure I'd find her crumpled in the dirt, instead, she was crawling through the fence. I grabbed her arm and tried to pull her back.

"Mother, what are you doing?"

"I'm going to Ventura. Now let go of me," she said, jerking her arm free.

"Mother, do you know how far away that is? You can't walk to Ventura."

"Oh yes I can."

She straightened up on the other side of the fence and wrenched Katie through. She continued her march down our country road, Katie dutifully walking beside her. I climbed through the fence, yelling for my husband, but he didn't hear me. I didn't have my cell phone and I couldn't leave mother alone, so I followed, trying to steady her as she walked. She yanked her arm away and pressed on. I tried to tell her how far it was to Ventura (more than an hour by car), but she wouldn't talk or look at me. She had the resolution of a general advancing to war. I was amazed she had so much strength, when only days before, she tottered from room to room. About a quarter of a mile later, she walked to the side of the road and sat down in the tall weeds.

"Mother there could be snakes in there."

"Good! Maybe one will bite me and I'll die," she said.

I felt so sorry for her and I didn't know how to make things okay.

We sat there a while. I was wondering how I could get her home when I spotted a car coming down the road. It was my son and daughter.

"Grammie? Mom? What are you doing in the weeds?"

"She wants to go to Ventura," I said.

"Come on Grammie. I'll take you home," my son said. Mother climbed in the car. I could see she was completely exhausted. He drove us back to the guest house. She sat down in the chair and was instantly asleep.

Chapter 12

Living at the Guest House

My life revolved around mother now. We had the stove in the guest house disabled as well as the microwave. No medications or vitamins of any kind, no scissors, no sharp knives, no matches, nothing that she could hurt herself with. We installed a monitor so we could see her in the living room and part of the kitchen. If she was out of view for a while I'd go see if she was okay. It helped me with my anxiety of not knowing what she was up to.

I cooked all of her meals. She wanted oatmeal in the morning, and if I tried to vary it with eggs or pancakes, she wouldn't eat, even her Wheaties, Breakfast of Champs, was out of her favor. Lunch was a sandwich or soup, milk and cookies. Most of it she gave to Katie to eat. I stocked her refrigerator with juices and snacks, and sometimes she'd take something, but mostly I had to offer it first and she'd only accept the drinks. She would eat cookies on her own, if I left them out on the counter.

Dinner was whatever I made for my husband and me. Mother refused to come to our house to eat, she preferred Katie's company.

The first week I took a watered-down bottle of Chardonnay to her so she could have a glass of wine with her dinner. She'd only accept a small glass. She'd changed so quickly from a bottle a day to barely a glass.

After a couple of days, she thought the apple juice in the refrigerator was wine. So I poured apple juice, right out of the juice bottle, in a small wine glass for her. She sipped it with her little pinky up.

Dinners were difficult. Mother picked at her food, more interested in feeding Katie, than herself.

"Mother, don't let Katie eat off your fork," I said. It became my nightly mantra. She ignored me. That's one thing she did well. I should have walked away, but I didn't. Stupidly, I persisted.

"Mother, please. That's icky."

She scooped up a handful of food and threw it at me. It always stunned me when she did things like that. Mean things. In my mind I was trying to be a good daughter, why didn't she see that? I cried all the time. What I didn't realize, or maybe what I didn't want to see, was that dementia was claiming her inch by inch, day by day. There wasn't much of her real self left.

Looking back, I wish that I'd picked my battles more wisely. What difference did it make if she and Katie shared the same fork? Matches and knives, things that she could hurt herself with were important, not a few dog germs or even eating a proper meal.

Mother always locked her front door so I'd knock and wait until she answered. I think it made her feel like she was in control but I had a key hidden so I could let myself in if she didn't respond. One morning my husband took mother her breakfast. He was back in a hurry. "She answered the door in a tee shirt," he said, "only a tee shirt."

I went over, "Mother, you can't answer the door without your pants on."

"Well," she said, "Ron didn't seem to mind."

Mother could still dress herself but sometimes she needed help.

"What are you wearing?" I asked one morning.

"It's my skirt."

"Mother, that's a blouse. "

She sneered at me. "No, it isn't."

I had to hire caregivers whenever I left the house. They were expensive and mother never liked them. Luckily, I had a few friends who volunteered to do it now and then and she enjoyed those visits if we kept them short.

I still took mother out for lunch several times a week. One day when we returned, I pushed the button to open our gate, drove through and jumped out to get the mail. Mother got out too, but I didn't see her. I was opening the car door to get back in, when I saw her walking out the gate just as it was closing. I quickly got through the gate and took her arm.

"Come on Mom, let's go back to the car."

"No," she said, and sat down in the driveway.

Nothing I could do or say, would make her budge. A neighbor I didn't know drove by. She stopped when she saw mother on the ground and asked me if she was okay. I smiled and said she was fine. She looked at mother, who looked pretty pathetic, and then back at me as she slowly drove off. The next neighbor that drove by knew me well and knew my mother. She stopped and together we tried to get mother up on her feet. But we couldn't do it. It felt like she was bolted to the driveway.

Finally, I called Ron at work on my cell phone. He said he would come right home. By the time he arrived several other neighbors had stopped to ask if I was sure mother was okay.

When Ron got home we were able to pick her up and put her into the car. I never knew why she did that and luckily it never happened again.

Marietta, mother's childhood friend from Nebraska, came every year to visit her son in Malibu. I'd always take mother to see her, and the three of us would go out to lunch. Since mother was living with us now, I asked Marietta if she'd like to come and stay a couple of days with her. Marietta hadn't been around mother since her dementia had begun, but I thought they'd get along fine for a couple of days. I also had an ulterior motive. Marietta was blind, but she was sharp as a tack, and I thought that if they got along then maybe Marietta would come and live in the guest house with mother. That way, Marietta could alert me to any problems with mother, and I could look after Marietta. I picked Marietta up from her son's house and we talked all the way home. Mother seemed to remember Marietta and she answered questions, but she didn't offer much to the conversation. We all had dinner together at the guest house and Marietta talked about their old friends. Mother seemed to be in good spirits so I left them for the night.

When I got to the guesthouse the next morning, I could see that Marietta was upset. She told me that mother had gone into her room several times during the night yelling and cussing obscenities. She thought mother was going to hit her. She was frightened and didn't get much sleep. I could see my plan wasn't going to work. I felt horrible that I'd put Marietta through such a terrible night, I had no idea mother would be that way to her old friend. I took Marietta back to my house and the two of us spent the day together.

Mother asked me all the time about the three nuns and a man who lived in the house across the street.

"That's my house, mother, and it's just across the driveway. Ron and I are the only ones who live there."

"No, Trudy, I know what I see. What does that man want with those nuns? They're in and out of the house all day long."

"Mother that's my house. Come with me and I'll show you."

"No way Trudy. That's not your house." She shook her head and gave me a look like I was delusional.

Chapter 13

The Bath

OUR BIGGEST CLASH CAME over bathing. She had been with us about two months and had never taken a shower or a bath. I'd worried about having to talk to her about it, but she clearly needed one. Her hair was beginning to smell and her fingernails were dirty.

"How about a nice bath today?" I said.

"I'm fine, leave me alone."

"You'll feel so much better."

"You'll feel so much better," she mimicked.

"Mother!"

"Mother!" She repeated.

The next day I suggested a bath with bubbles. "Won't that feel good?"

"No."

"Pleassssse."

"No way, Trudy."

Finally, after a week of pleading, I said. "You are going to have a bath today."

"No, I'm not."

"Oh yes you are."

I tried to help her out of her nightgown. We struggled. I won, sort of.

"Mother, please stop fighting me. It will feel good to get clean."

"Nooooo," she yelled.

She dragged her long fingernails down my arm, drawing lines of blood.

"Mother!"

I'd gotten her nightgown off and I wasn't going to back down now. I put my arm around her waist and tried to walk her into the bathroom, but she sank to the floor screaming at me. I slid her along the floor. She grabbed at everything and finally got ahold of a tennis shoe. She slapped me in the head with it all the way to the tub. Mother was strong when she was mad.

When I got her into the warm bath, she cupped her hands and threw water in my face and screamed, "Bitch," at the top of her lungs.

"Stop it." I screamed back, struggling to shampoo her hair.

When we were done, mother looked great. She seemed happy and refreshed. She sat down to read the paper. Mascara smeared my eyes. I resembled a raccoon. My wet clothes and hair clung to me. Water dripped from my shirt. I had fought a war, and I wasn't sure who had won. I went back to my house and bawled like a baby. How could that little woman upset me so?

It was 6 weeks before I suggested another bath. We repeated the same idiotic performance. After that I swore I'd never do it again.

Chapter 14

Mother Where Are Your Teeth?

ONE MORNING MOTHER TOLD me the toilet was clogged. The plumber found the problem, mother's glasses. They were bent up, but they weren't broken. I wanted to take her to get new glasses. She refused. She refused nearly anything I wanted her to do, like my kids, when they were two years old. At least with my kids I could pick them up and go. Not so with my spit-fire mother. So I cleaned her glasses and she put them back on. I wondered how they ended up in the toilet. I didn't ask.

Some days later, I found the newspaper folded up nicely in the toilet. Luckily she hadn't tried to flush . . . or had she? I fished it out. The next day I found her shoe in the toilet and after that sheets, dishes, all sorts of things. It was her place of choice. So each morning I'd check the toilet before anything else. One day I couldn't find her teeth. I hadn't seen them in the toilet.

"Mother where are your teeth?" She looked up at me and shrugged. I looked in her pockets, the wastebaskets, cupboards, and her drawers. I felt under furniture, inside vases, in shoes, everywhere I could think of. I charged through the house. I was on a mission. They had to be here. I opened the door to get some air and that's when I saw Katie gnawing on something on the lawn. Of course—her teeth. They were still intact. Katie hadn't broken through the shield of Fixodent, nor had the worms that clung there.

I put on rubber gloves and flicked the worms off. I brushed the teeth under a stream of hot water and soap, repeating to myself, don't think, don't think, don't think. I couldn't scrub the Fixodent off so I resorted to my husband's screw driver and pliers. When that didn't work, I called my cousin Steve, the dentist.

"Yeah, the screw driver is what I use, works pretty good," he said.

It took me hours to get them to where I could look at them without gagging.

Mother never wore her teeth again. She hadn't seen the worms. She refused to go to the dentist for new ones, no matter how much I begged. She had one bottom tooth left in her mouth. I asked her if it was hard to chew. She looked at me like I was nuts. Sometimes, after chewing for long time, she'd pull something out of her mouth and give it to Katie. But this was nothing, compared with what was to come.

Chapter 15

Hair Incident

ONE MORNING, RON VENTURED over to the guest house with breakfast for mother. She was in the bathroom. He knocked on the door and told her breakfast was ready. She yelled at him to go away.

"You better go check on your mother," he said when he got back to our house. "Something's not right."

When I knocked on the bathroom door, she shrieked, "Leave!"

I gave her more time. Then, I politely asked, "Is everything okay, Mother?"

"I'm fine Trudy. Leave me alone!"

I sat down and waited.

Finally, the door opened and she came out with Katie following behind. My mother had a beautiful head of snow white hair, but this morning there was a reddish brown streak down the middle of her head. She was smiling as she walked toward me.

"Mother, what's in your hair?"

She didn't say anything, but as she got closer, I smelled it.

I got on the phone and called my house. When my husband answered, I said, "Come over now! Mother put poop in her hair."

"What's in her hair?"

"Poop."

"I'm sorry, honey, but I don't understand what you're saying," he said.

"She put shit in her hair. Shit! Shit! Shit! Do you understand me now? Mother put shit in her hair!"

"I'll be right there," he said.

Seeing my mother like this slammed me head first into awareness of how far away she had gone. I wanted to curl up into a ball and wish this all away, but no amount of wishing would change it.

I pushed mother towards the kitchen sink. She tried to resist but I shoved her head under the water and poured dish soap over her head.

Our kids were at our house visiting, so Ron brought his middle daughter, Katrine, who is a nurse with him. My husband took one look at mother's hair and gagged.

"Go home Dad," Katrine said. "I've got this covered."

She went into the bathroom. Mother's comb was pressed into her feces on the counter. The drawers and cupboards had segments of excrement too.

Katrine cleaned up the bathroom, something I'm not sure the rest of us could have done. It wasn't even lunch time and it seemed a lifetime had passed. In a way, it had.

Chapter 16

Move to Nursing Home

THE NEXT DAY KATRINE volunteered to stay with Mother while Ron had eye surgery at UCLA. It was an outpatient procedure and we'd be back before dinner.

On our way home Katrine called to tell us grammie had fallen. She suspected a broken pelvis. She had a nasty gash on her arm as well, which Katrine had cleaned and bandaged. She said she would call 911, but if we were home soon, she'd rather wait. She thought the ambulance would freak grammie out. We agreed.

I called mother's doctor and he told me to take her to emergency for an X-ray as soon as we got home. Katrine was right, it was a hairline fracture of her pelvis. Her doctor wanted to get her into the local nursing home, but they couldn't take her until the next day. We brought her home and I moved into the guest house to care for her.

She was in pain but refused Advil or aspirin, saying she'd already taken some. She hadn't. I couldn't cajole her into taking anything, no matter what I said. It was terrible seeing how much pain she was in, yet I was powerless to do anything.

We borrowed a wheelchair for her but we still had to help her to the bathroom and into bed. Ron was not allowed to lift anything over five pounds after his surgery, so it was up to me. She was a dead weight. I feared my back would give out every time I moved her, and she groaned in pain with the slightest contact.

The following day, my son came up to help me take mother to the nursing home. I was breaking the vow I'd made to myself about putting her in a home, but what could I do? I told her that we were taking her to a nursing home so she could get better. She didn't argue, but when we arrived, she said she wouldn't get out of the car.

"I'll die if I have to stay here."

"Now grammie," my son said, "just give it a try."

"You know I love you Nicky, but if you touch me, I'll kick you in the balls."

We were at a crossroads again.

I went inside.

"My mother won't get out of the car," I said to the woman at the front desk.

"Don't worry, we'll get her." She gave me a warm smile.

My mouth was dry. I was nauseated and I hated myself for what I was doing. The thought—I'm abandoning my mother—looped my brain.

Jan, a nurse on duty, said, "I know this is hard, but it's going to be okay. You're doing the right thing. You can come by day or night, anytime you want to see your mother. You'll see," she said, patting my arm, "in two weeks she'll be used to us and we'll know how to please her."

I filled out the admission papers in a blur. When I returned to the lobby I was surprised to see mother there. How did they get her out of the car? I walked with her to her new room and then the nurse told me I should leave and come back after they got her settled.

The next day I went early to see mother. She looked clean and rosy-cheeked. My mouth dropped open. Later Jan told me that mother had refused the bath that they give everyone who moves in. "I told her, you can fight us, or you can cooperate, it's your choice. Either way, we are going to bathe you."

Mother decided to cooperate, and in the end, she loved it. It was a big whirlpool with lots of bubbles.

About two weeks later, I saw an improvement in her. The nurses had been able to get her to take her meds, one thing she would never do for me. She seemed happy and talked to everyone who passed by.

Mother hadn't asked me about her dog Katie yet, which I had given away to a friend, because I knew that my mother would not be leaving the nursing home. Each day, I wondered when the realization that her dog wasn't around would hit her. I brooded over what I would say when she asked. She never asked.

When guests brought dogs to visit, mother would pet them and tell the them about Katie, as if she was in the next room, but that's as far as it went.

Meals were tasty and mother was eating almost everything, which surprised me since she had had such a limited preference of food before.

After a couple of months our relationship improved. Mother seemed at home, which made me think that I'd made the right decision. I relaxed, a little.

One day a nurse told me, "It takes so many of us to care for Helen. When one of us can't negotiate with her, there are others who take over, and, we have a day shift and a night shift. We just can't imagine how you managed alone."

That was priceless validation. I did have my husband's help, but most of the caregiving and emotional worry was mine. I don't know how much longer I could have done it. Luckily I didn't have to find out, and from the looks of mother, both of us had benefited.

Chapter 17

Life at the Nursing Home

As the weeks went by, I saw mother most everyday except the weekends. I got to know the residents and the staff. Things that had upset me before, like seeing people sitting in the hall, didn't bother me anymore. I saw deeper into things. I saw the kindheartedness and patience of the caregivers. For example, one day I walked in and heard screams from a room down the hall.

"Oh oh," I said to a caregiver, "is that my mother?" She nodded.

I went to mother's room. She was on the toilet screaming and swiping at the two caregivers who were holding her so she wouldn't fall.

"Mother, stop screaming, they're only trying to help you."

"Well, they're bitches and I don't need their help."

She resumed her screaming and didn't stop until the caregivers got her tidied up and back into her wheelchair. Then mother looked at me and grinned, sweet as a lollipop. I apologized to the young women who had taken her abuse. They just laughed and told me not to worry. "We love your mom; she has spunk."

One morning I got a call from the nursing home. The nurse said mother had refused breakfast because she didn't have money to pay for it. They assured her it had already been taken care of. Still, she wouldn't eat. So they made copies of five, ten, and twenty dollar bills on green paper, and cut them out. They slipped the bills into a little purse and gave it to her. She was thrilled and couldn't wait to show me her money. She counted the money out in piles, over and over. It made me happy that she could still count correctly. When I tried to look at one of the bills she snatched it out of my hand.

"Don't you trust me, mother?"

"Nope," she said, gathering her loot back in her purse.

For years my mother's friends had always said, "Your mother is so funny."

"My mother?" I wondered who they were talking about. I never saw anything funny about her, until now. Now she made me laugh, but her humor could turn into anger without warning. At least now I could walk away and let the caregivers deal with her nasty side.

"Wait until you see what your mom is doing today," Uni, the young woman at the front desk, said.

"Is it bad?"

She shook her head, "No, funny. She's in the dining room. Go see."

From across the room, I saw mother in her wheelchair taking a long drag on a drinking straw. She'd finally found her cigarette. The caregivers had colored one end with a red pen to make it look like it was burning ash. When she'd asked for a light, they'd click their ball point pen under her straw and mother would suck in.

Later, Julie, one of the nurses bought her a cigarette from a magic store. If you blew, powder came out the end. It looked like smoke. It was so real looking in fact, that one of the guests who was visiting, yanked it out of mother's hand and marched up to the front desk indignant, demanding the nurses do a better job policing their wards.

Invariably, when I went to visit mother, I heard some funny story about her. This day the story was that they'd had a staff meeting in the nurse's office. My mother rolled her wheelchair into the meeting as if she belonged. Instead of sending her out, they went on with the meeting. After discussing their business, a nurse turned to my mother and asked if she had anything to add.

"Nope, you did a real good job honey," she said.

The nurses realized the meeting had made mother feel important. So they decided to give her a job as a greeter, because she said, "Hi 'dare," to everyone she saw. She nearly burst with pride when they pinned the "Official Greeter" badge on her. They told me later the job went straight to her head. She became a supervisor overnight, yelling, "Get back to work, and stop goofing off," at anyone she thought wasn't busy enough.

One afternoon when I was leaving, I said, "I love you, mother."

"I love you too sweetie, now cut the crap, and leave me alone."

Often mother would scoot her wheelchair up to the front desk and order a whiskey. Or she'd tell the nurses that she had been a prostitute in Ventura, working under the bridge by the river, but she had to quit because she didn't make any money.

One day she got inside the reception area before I could stop her. I told her that she shouldn't be there and to come out. She ignored me. The nurse told me it was okay, not to worry. Mother proceeded to go through all the drawers looking into everything. I was getting anxious but the nurses reassured me by their smiles that all was okay, even when she started tearing pages out of the phone book. I realized that she hadn't done any real harm and it gave her a sense of importance. I loved the nurses for being so easy with her and when I tried to thank them they would tell me, "Our residents are our number one priority. Besides we get a kick out of your mom, she's so funny."

Mother and I were sitting opposite each other, visiting, when she leaned toward me and touched my arm. Looking back at me was my coherent mother. She looked directly into my eyes and said, "Will you remember?"

"Remember," I stuttered, "that you're my mother?"

"Yes," she said.

She was tender and sweet, sweeter than I can ever remember her being to me in my entire life.

I choked, "Of course, I'll remember. You're my mother. I'll never forget you. I love you."

"I can't remember things," she said. "It's like my mind won't hold onto anything anymore."

"Does that frighten you?" I asked.

"Of course it does," she said. Then suddenly, her eyes glazed over, she leaned back in her wheelchair and disappeared into the fog of dementia. I sat there a moment barely breathing, waiting to see if she might come back. She didn't. I felt like a rope was wrapped around my throat holding back a flood of emotion. I found a nurse on duty and choked-out the story to her.

"She had a moment of clarity," she said. "It happens sometimes."

"It was so sad," I said, wiping at my tears.

"I know," she said, and reached over and hugged me.

At times mother would be agitated because she thought someone had left a baby and she needed to get it. I'd try to distract her, but she kept repeating, "Get my purse Trudy. Get the car. Let's go." To calm her down I had to wheel her out the front door of the nursing home before something would distract her, and she'd forget her mission.

In the dining room one day, she pointed to a woman and said. "That is the ugliest hat I've ever seen." Her voice boomed, like it was coming through a loudspeaker.

"Mother," I whispered, "that's the woman's hair."

"Well, it's still ugly," she said.

It was hard to sit with her during mealtimes because she'd mix all of her food together: mashed potatoes, meatloaf, corn, Jell-O, pudding, soup, and milk. One day, her tablemate commented on the concoction and mother picked up a glass of water and threw it at her, glass and all. She was moved to another table. No one commented on her food after that.

Other times, mother was helpful, alerting caregivers to someone who had dropped something or was having a hard time. Or she'd pat someone on the back as she rolled by in her wheelchair saying, "Hi 'dare." She did this one day to a man who was also in a wheelchair as we passed by. The man took a swing at her but missed, because his personal caregiver pulled him back instantly. The incident didn't register with mother at all. She was still chattering at him while his caregiver apologized to me. I'd wondered why a personal caregiver was next to him at all times.

What most people see when they first walk into a nursing home is surface stuff. Old people in wheelchairs lined up in the hall, and yes, a slight smell of urine, because someone in that line is sure to have just soiled their Depends. But before mother moved into the nursing home, she slept in her chair during the day and accidents happened there too.

Another criticism that I've heard is that everyone is in a wheelchair, which is mostly true. But there is a good reason. When mother broke her pelvis she had to be in a wheelchair. After it healed they gave her physical therapy, which she did twice and then refused to do anymore. With her dementia she was forgetting how to walk. There was a rail on the side of the hall for people to hold while they were walking. But many, including mother, had lost the concept of holding onto it for balance, so it was of no help. So even though a person looks able to walk and has no physical issues, they end up falling because they don't have the understanding of how to do it anymore.

Life spun around mother in the nursing home. Even if she didn't participate, she always had something to watch. It enlivened her. Often, she would park her wheelchair next to a gentleman in the hall. She'd get his leg up on her lap and take off his sock. The trouble was that the man's wife was also living there. The wife didn't like her husband and wouldn't give him the time of day, yet she didn't want my mother near him. So the nurses were on alert when they saw her coming and would move mother away to avoid marital problems, or worse.

One day a maintenance man walked by a resident sitting in the hall. She reached out to him and told him that she didn't know if she was in the right place. She was confused and didn't know where to go. The man told her that he gets that way sometimes too, and that she shouldn't worry, because it happens to everyone. He spent twenty minutes talking to her until she brightened up and was laughing. Then he offered to show her where her room was. I was near tears at the way he connected with this woman. A little kindness goes a long way.

I had a picture of mother taken on her eighty-eighth birthday with a bouquet of balloons tied on the back of her wheelchair. Between hot pink fingernails she held her make-believe cigarette. Her eyebrows were raised into upside down v's, which seemed to pull her whole face up into a whimsical grin. I couldn't believe this was the same person who was so belligerent living in my guest house, or her house for that matter.

People say, "I'd never put my parent in a nursing home." I felt that way too, until I had no choice. But, I got lucky. What I experienced was laughter, life, and love. There was sadness too, but that was when someone passed away, was sick, or upset. Those are normal responses. The nursing home was not sad. Everyone on staff had time to stop and say a kind word or tell a joke or admire a new hair do. There were kisses and hugs too. I was brought to tears many times with the kindness that I witnessed.

Chapter 18

Wound Doctor

MOTHER REFUSED TO WEAR shoes or slippers. I didn't want her roaming around the nursing home without something on her feet, so I bought her socks. She'd wear them some of the time, but mostly she wouldn't. I bought her all kinds of quirky socks to entice her. Some that looked like cows, others with big eyes and ears, hearts and flowers, anything I thought she'd find appealing. She'd wear them for a little while and then she'd pull them off and drape them on chairs, as she inched her way down the hall in her wheelchair using her feet to move. She'd forgotten how to push the wheels on the wheelchair with her hands and arms. I showed her over and over, but it wouldn't stick in her mind.

Her circulation was poor and her feet and legs were always cold. It didn't seem to bother her. One day she got a nick on her little toe. It healed, and then she got another one. The second one didn't get better. Her doctor thought it was gangrene. He wanted her to see a wound specialist in Santa Barbara, a town 45 minutes south of us.

The nursing home had a small bus that we could wheel mother's chair into and secure. Her favorite caregiver, Marcello, would be driving. I was worried about the trip because mother was unpredictable. What if she panicked and tried to get out? Or she might scream all the way there. I never knew what she would do.

We were just pulling away from the nursing home when Julie, one of the nurses, ran out and jumped on the bus with us. I was relieved. I had a hard time controlling mother, but Julie and Marcello had the powers of persuasion with her. The drive was uneventful and she seemed to enjoy herself.

When we arrived at the office, the nurses settled mother into a chaise lounge, and rolled her pant leg up. I was shocked at the dramatic change in her foot, from just the day before. Now her leg was an angry red to her mid-calf.

The doctor was a big guy, in his thirties. He introduced himself to Mother, who was in good humor. I relaxed. She was cooperating today. The doctor examined her. "Your mother has gangrene in her toe and it's spreading up her leg."

My breath skipped, though it was obvious.

"We need to schedule an operation immediately, to amputate her leg from the knee down." He said it like you might tell someone to remove their jacket. He said it in front of my mother. She must not have understood because her expression didn't change.

I stared at him. "Take her leg off? Her eighty-nine-year-old leg?"

"Yes."

"How do you plan to keep my mother in a hospital bed? She has dementia. You can't really control her." I heard the panic in my voice.

"She'll have to be restrained," he said matter-of-factly.

My thoughts raced. Mother had dementia, she was not up to this. Years earlier she had had an operation because of a clogged artery. She didn't show signs of dementia then, at least nothing that I or her doctor detected. In recovery they had to restrain her because she was tearing the tubes out and trying to get out of bed. They couldn't handle her and called me to help.

When I arrived she was wild-eyed. Her wrists and ankles were strapped to the bed. She whispered something and I leaned in to hear her. She told me there was a letter under her covers. I pulled out a scrap of paper from a note pad. It was a child's scrawl, not my mother's beautiful handwriting. "Call 911 I'm being held against my will!" She writhed in her bed trying to free herself and whispered that they were trying to kill her.

"Oh no, mother," I said, wanting to soothe her, "they aren't trying to kill you, they are the doctors and nurses. They're here to help you."

"I knew you wouldn't believe me," she spat, turning her head from side to side and pulling at the restraints.

I made a big mistake that day, one I still regret. I should have agreed with her and made up a story that would have comforted her instead of trying to make her accept my reality.

Now she was ten years older, with dementia. What would amputating her leg do to her?

"I just don't understand how this will work," I said. "She doesn't like to stay in one place for very long. You got her on a good day."

"Well, if we don't amputate, she'll die," he said.

I couldn't speak. My brain scrambled to understand.

"If it was my mother, I'd do it," he said.

But your mother isn't her age, I said, or thought, I'm not sure which.

I felt assaulted. What was the right thing to do? If I didn't have her leg amputated, then I was signing her death certificate. But how could I put her through something so drastic?

The doctor was called out of the room.

"Trudy, you don't have to do this," Julie said, "you don't have to make a decision this moment. Why don't you call Terry and talk it over with her?"

Julie woke me up to my own power. I didn't have to decide this moment nor did I have to do what the doctor wanted.

I went into the hall to call Terry, the head nurse at mother's nursing home.

"What do you want to do?" Terry asked.

"I just can't imagine amputating Mother's leg at this point in her life. She's confused now, what would that do to her? I see no good reason to put her through it. Even if she didn't have gangrene we all know she's nearing the end of her life."

"Do you want her to go into the hospital?"

"No, I want her to go back to her room, where it's familiar to her. I want all of you, who know and understand her, to care for her until the end."

"We can do that," she said softly.

I wiped at my tears.

"I'd like to call hospice to help us through her dying process," Terry said.

Dying process . . . ? "Yes, of course," I whispered, "thank you."

I turned my cell phone off and slumped against the wall. I must have been holding my breath because I suddenly exhaled and a juggernaut of raw and primal emotions ripped open inside me. I howled for my mother, for the decision I was making, and for myself. It took me sometime before I could face anyone.

When I went back to the exam room, I felt better. I'd made a decision, one I hoped mother would have wanted. We all die and when we are only a shell of ourselves, is it really living? Life at all costs seems cruel.

When I told the doctor my decision, he softened. "You're making the right decision," he said. "Here's my card." He looked me in the eye, "Call me anytime."

His voice was tender and I knew he meant it.

Chapter 19

Dying

THE WOUND DOCTOR TOLD me that gangrene moves quickly. He said hospice would manage the pain and it wasn't a bad way to go. I didn't take my eyes off of mother. I wasn't sure what "quickly" meant.

The next day she seemed her usual self. A bicycle race came through our town three days later. Mother felt good, so the caregivers took her out to the street to watch the riders go by.

A few days later she was in bed. Hospice had started and everyone was on high alert. We'd had hospice for my mother-in-law when she passed away, so I knew the gift they offer. They don't fight the dying process. Their focus is to manage pain and make the patient and their families as comfortable as possible until the end comes. The hospice nurse said it wouldn't be long. But when I called the nursing home the following morning, they told me mother was in the dining room, wearing a hat made from the newspaper.

I went right over. Mother was sitting in her wheelchair in a blue flowered blouse, black pants, and a paper hat. She looked proud with her paper hat perched on top of her head. She called it her hard hat. She was full of energy that day and for the next couple of days too. But then she was back in bed again. This time it was for good.

In her delirium she spoke aloud to Betsy, my mother-in-law who had passed away nine years earlier. My husband has often witnessed those who have passed over, coming to the bedside of the dying. This day he saw his mother. She was telling my mother not to be afraid that she would help her over. Ron told me she reached out for my mother's hand, but mother wouldn't go. She was not ready.

Ron sat by her bed, telling her that there was nothing to fear. She kept her eyes closed, but he knew she could hear him, because tears slid down her cheek.

Our kids came to see her to say their goodbyes. She was unresponsive to everyone except my son, Nick. He didn't say much to her, he just sat and held her hand, his face inches from hers. She looked at him with the trusting eyes of a child. Now and then, a tear would slip down her cheek.

The entire staff at the nursing home was engaged in our process, bringing tea, cookies, sweet words, whatever kindness they could think of. When they tended my mother their touch was gentle, as if it was their own mother they served. I wanted to tell them how much they were appreciated, but when I tried to speak, their eyes held so much concern, that I turned away, fearing my emotions would overwhelm me. I could see this wasn't easy for them either. How many times had they watched one of their residents die?

I remembered back to when mother had been in the nursing home only a few days. Someone had passed away and the family and nurses had gathered in the living room, along with a priest, to remember her. Everyone was invited, and even though we hadn't known the woman, I took mother.

A nurse dabbed at her eyes as she spoke about the resident.

"Every morning when I went into Mrs. Green's room, she would smile and say, 'This is the day the Lord has made let us rejoice and be glad.' If I was feeling down, hearing her greeting always snapped me out of it. She was so happy and positive about life. I will miss her."

Many others spoke about Mrs. Green that day, and I was touched because I saw how much the staff cared about their residents. I understood better after mother had been there a year or so, because I found my feelings getting tangled up in these old folks too.

The end was drawing near for mother. I didn't want to leave her side. Two of our daughters had come to make us dinner at our house. The nurses told Ron and me to go home and eat and they would sit in mother's room and call if there was a change. I ate quickly. When the phone rang, I jumped for it. She was gone.

My daughters and I hurried back to the nursing home. I stood at the foot of the bed. Her body was still there, but "she" was elsewhere. There was a feeling of peace in the room. Mother's struggle was finally over. She was free of her worn-out body and mind. It had been twenty-two days since the visit with the wound doctor.

I washed mother's body with water and rose oil and the girls helped me dress her in the white satin pajamas that I had brought for her. I combed her hair. We sprinkled rose petals over her body from a bouquet I'd picked that morning from our yard. I took pictures. I didn't cry. It was evening. Everything was quiet. We went home. For the first time in my life, I didn't have a mother. I felt disconnected, odd.

I had wanted to witness the moment that mother's spirit left her body, but I was pretty sure she wouldn't let me be there. It's hard to say goodbye for a long trip, harder for a lifetime.

After her husband died, mother and I had about six good years before dementia claimed her totally. When it did, we slid down a dark hole, confused at the new world we tumbled in. Her mind was being cleaned of memories and paths that she had traveled her whole life. I was trying to save her, to steer her back to normal, to stop this trajectory she was on. It was impossible.

Chapter 20

The Memorial

Mother told me years earlier that she didn't want a church service after she died. She was the only one left of her six siblings and most of her friends were gone as well.

"Just cremate me and sprinkle my ashes," she said.

I wanted to do something to mark her passage from this world. I decided to have a memorial for mother at the nursing home. I hired a restaurant to cater lunch and invited everyone who worked there, plus our family and friends. I'd set the time for two in the afternoon, to accommodate both shifts. It was a way to say thank you to all of the people who'd cared for her in her last years. We set up tables in the living room with linens and flowers.

On a round table, I placed pictures of mother during her life, beginning when she was a young girl, to her latest pictures in the nursing home. Years before, I'd knitted her a pink hat and purse. Most of the presents I got for her, I found still in boxes after I moved her to my house. But I knew she loved the hat and purse, because she wore them all the time. I placed those on the table alongside an ashtray with her make-believe cigarette. I splayed out her play money next to the little purse the nurses had given her.

One of the female resident's daily routine was to nap on the sofa in the living room. In the mist of our celebration, she slept peacefully without making a sound. One of my friends told me later, that she was taken aback when she first saw her thinking it was my mother laid out for a wake.

Another friend, who did not see the sleeping woman under the blanket, was about to sit down on her, when I managed to grab his arm and pull him away.

It warmed my heart having these little whimsies at mother's memorial. I know she would have gotten a kick out of them.

During lunch I thanked the staff for the care and kindness they'd given my mother and our family over the years. I shared stories about her life. One, that I related happened years before, when I asked her what she believed would happened when we die.

"We go to heaven."

"What is heaven like?" I asked.

She took a minute to think, "Well, it isn't Ventura."

When I finished, I invited others to share their stories. There were many stories that day and most of them funny.

I think almost everyone came up to me, at one time or another, to say how much they would miss Helen.

It was a sweet closure to mother's life.

Chapter 21

What I Learned

DON'T ARGUE. YOUR PARENT'S reality isn't yours, nor is it what theirs used to be before dementia changed them. They will never see things logically, no matter how many examples you give them, or how hard you try to explain. So give it up, the sooner the better. Agree with them or distract them, then take care of business.

If they're driving when you know they shouldn't be, then you have to do the right thing, no matter how much it might upset them. It's for their safety and the safety of others. If you have a creative side make up a story. One of my friends told her mother that her daughter's car had broken down, and she needed to borrow Nana's car. Of course the car never came back, but her mother had forgotten it by then. That story saved a lot of grief for everyone.

If your parent tells you that a friend or relative has stolen from them, and you're sure that's not the case, sympathize and move quickly onto another subject. Or, if they tell you that their doctor is trying to kill them, don't try to convince them otherwise, show concern and then, if you can, devise a story that will make them feel safe. It's easy to get caught up your parent's distress; changing the subject is like a magic eraser. Remember to use it often.

Be compassionate. Battling with my mother everyday overwhelmed me so completely that compassion was present only in the middle of the night as I stared at the ceiling. I'd promise myself every morning that I'd be more understanding, but it's hard to be compassionate with someone who is challenging you at every turn. It wasn't until mother went into a nursing home and I didn't have the responsibility to care for her 24/7, that I was able to find my compassion. She battled the caregivers, screamed and yelled at them, but she was not their mother and they didn't take it personally.

They can't help it. It's hard to believe that your parent isn't just being mean or difficult, because at times they seem normal. It is hard because we are so bound up with them emotionally. We have to switch roles and become their parent and help them through this rugged time of their lives.

They won't notice. I worried years off of my life when I took away mother's dog and her cigarettes, but neither of those things ever became issues. So save your worries for what is on your plate at the moment, and not what you think might come.

Take care of yourself. Taking care of a parent with dementia is a demanding undertaking. You might have promised your parent that you would always care for them at home. However, promising a coherent parent, and promising a parent with a disorder of the mind, are two different things. One day my husband said that he was worried that I was the one who was going to end up in a nursing home. You might not notice that you are sliding down hill, but your friends and family will. Believe them when they tell you. Getting sick yourself won't help your parent, yourself, or your family.

Don't feel guilty. Feeling guilty about aging parents is an easy feeling to adopt. This is all uncharted territory, even if you've been through it before with someone else, because dementia can present itself differently in each person. And, believe it or not, you are not super human. All you can do is your best. Believe that, and don't listen to your inner judge.

Feeling guilty doesn't help the situation in anyway, but it will wear you down.

Get help. Getting help for your parent can be costly. Not everyone can afford it. If you can afford it, do it. That doesn't mean you have to go as far as a nursing home. You can hire people to clean, cook, or sit with your parent. Anything that will cut down on your responsibilities will cut down on your stress. If you don't have financial resources, maybe your parent does. In my case we had to sell mother's house to pay for the nursing home. If you don't have resources then ask a friend to come for an hour, now and then, to relieve you. In some cities there are inexpensive senior care programs available, that might be helpful for an afternoon. Even a little respite is beneficial.

Look for a support group. You won't feel so alone and you will learn things from other people's experiences and knowledge. If you can't find a group, find a therapist. This will help enormously. Some therapy is covered by insurance and some charge by a sliding scale. If neither of those is an option, pay for it yourself, it's worth your sanity and your health.

Durable Power of Attorney and Health Directive: Get these done ASAP. They will be invaluable to you when you have to take over your parent's affairs.

Humor. If you find humor anywhere, lap it up.

If some of the incidents I've shared with you seem unkind to my mother's memory, I want you to know that I've thought long and hard about this. But to sugar coat my experience would be of no real help to you. Your experience will be different, and not all parents are difficult, some become more good-natured than they were before.

Dementia distorts the mind of those we love, and while it is sad and upsetting, there are also gifts that make their way into our hearts that might only have been achieved in this way.

Chapter 22

Where to Find Help

Internet

Alz.org is an amazing site for in-depth information on Alzheimer's and other dementias.

Google *hospice* to see what kind of care is in your area.

Books you might find helpful.

Facing The Final Mystery by Laura Larsen

Being Mortal: Medicine and What Matters in the End by Atul Gawande